Design Graphics

Drawing Techniques for Design Professionals

Written and Illustrated by

Peter A. Koenig
Florida State University

Prentice Hall
Upper Saddle River, New Jersey 07458

ublication Data

s for design professionals /
nig.

p. cm.
Includes bibliographical references
ISBN 0-13-742982-7
    1. Interior decoration rendering.   2. Architectual drawing—
Techniques.   3. Communication in architectural design.   I. Title.
NK2113.5.K64   2000
720'.28'4—dc21   99-42462
                                                            CIP

Acquisitions Editor: Elizabeth Sugg
Managing Editor: Mary Carnis
Director of Production and Manufacturing: Bruce Johnson
Editorial Production Services: WordCrafters Editorial Services, Inc.
Production Liaison: Eileen M. O'Sullivan
Manufacturing Manager: Ed O'Dougherty
Marketing Manager: Shannon Simonsen
Editorial Assistant: Delia Uherec
Interior Designer: Laura Cleveland
Cover Director: Jayne Conte
Cover Designer: Joe Sengotta
Printer/Binder: Victor Graphics

Printed in the United States of America
10 9 8 7 6 5 4 3 2 1

ISBN 0-13-742982-7

Prentice-Hall International (UK) Limited, *London*
Prentice-Hall of Australia Pty. Limited, *Sydney*
Prentice-Hall Canada, Inc., *Toronto*
Prentice-Hall Hispanoamericana, *Mexico*
Prentice-Hall of India Private Limited, *New Delhi*
Prentice-Hall of Japan, *Tokyo*
Prentice-Hall Pte., Ltd., *Singapore*
Editora Prentice-Hall do Brasil, Ltda., *Rio de Janeiro*

To my one and only **donalee**
our daughter **Moya**
Mom, thank you

CONTENTS

vi

PREFACE

This book evolved from a new course I developed in interior design graphics. I started my career as an interior designer and architectural renderer in New York City in 1969. I first taught graphics for interior designers in 1970. Over the years I have relied on texts by many graphic educators including Kirby Lockard, Edward T. White, and Paul Leaseau.

A number of choices were available to me as textbooks for my new course, but I soon realized I would need several that covered a great deal of nonrelated material. Most books on graphics attempt to be far too comprehensive and fail to meet specific needs. I then produced a booklet to meet my specific requirements based on my own professional experience and drawings. That booklet evolved into this book.

The three main areas of emphasis in this text are sketching, design drawing, and the drawing process. These are the most critical areas related to the designer's ability to design and communicate. The text takes a monochromatic approach since color technique is the subject of another course in our graphic series. However, the basics of this text are the foundation for success in color renderings.

The text is intended for interior design students but is pertinent for many other design students and professionals.

Intended as a primer-level book, it shows simple techniques and skills related to sketching, design development, and the schematic or preliminary phase of design presentation. These simple techniques are of great benefit to the professional.

It is ironic that although this course was developed to recognize the need for and maintain hand drawing as a *design skill, much of the initial layout and formatting was done with the help of the computer. In the age of computer-aided drawing (CAD), it is imperative that graphic communicators keep the skill of hand drawing alive. It has certainly proved to me that the drawing skills of the past can coexist with and be a beneficial part of the computer age.*

Many thanks for the valuable and enlightening comments from my esteemed colleagues: Ann Kellogg, Illinois Institute of Art; Nancy Kwallek, University of Texas at Austin; Christine Myres, University of Arkansas; David R. Pohl, University of Memphis; Maria Siera, University of Missouri; and Catherine St. John, Berkeley College.

I would like to thank David Butler, Bob Burke, Tim White, and Kirby Lockard for their help and inspiration in making this book become a reality.

Peter A. Koenig

PREFACE

Introduction
DRAWING

Why do we draw?

The most simplistic answer is clearly to communicate. Designers can try to communicate ideas verbally or with the written word, although we should not choose to emulate the poet or the novelist because ours is a visual art form.

Design graphics incorporates sections on sketching, design drawing, and the drawing process. Can these drawing skills be learned? The answer is a definitive YES. Artistic ability is a plus but not a necessity. Rather, a desire to learn and a willingness to practice, practice, practice are the keys to success.

In many cases, an awareness of reality or simply "learning to see" can be our guide. The average person is happy to process seeing into just not bumping into anything during the course of a day. This, however, is not the level of seeing one expects from a designer. Special concern for relationships, elements, and details is critical to the designer as observer.

In general, the mere act of drawing, physically putting lines and media on a surface, has survived throughout the ages. Clearly this skill is being threatened in the age of computer-aided drawing. Fortunately, drawing educators across the country not only believe the skill must be maintained but that it is a necessary foundation for the development of many computer-aided activities.

DRAWING FOR FUN

Sometimes designers draw or sketch just for the sheer emotional and physical pleasure of the experience.

DRAWING FOR DESIGN

In the preliminary or schematic phase of design, we are able to THINK through the use of our visual shorthand, drawing conceptual/doodle diagrams to examine potential solutions on paper. We draw to:

- *Record our ideas, rather than relying on our memory.*
- *Keep track of the evolution of ideas.*
- *Transfer ideas from our mind's eye that do not presently exist in a way that can represent future reality.*
- *Allow the expression of creativity.*
- *Allow for change before change becomes both costly and prohibitive.*
- *Acquire final client approval.*

DRAWING FOR COMMUNICATION

This is the skill of presenting design ideas, concepts, and solutions to a client. These drawings may vary in scope from a sketch, napkin art *over lunch, to a full-blown final-board presentation. The design process section of this text examines several presentation alternatives including the overlay method. These methods will vary and are always affected by time and budgetary constraints.*

Section One
SKETCHING

How do we define sketching?

The art of sketching is an expression of a style or technique of free-hand drawing. It is a skill generally learned by drawing what you see, relying on the development of hand/eye coordination.

A sketch may be:

- tight (Figure SK1.3) or loose (Figure SK1.2),
- line drawing only (Figure SK1.3), or
- any combination of line, tone/shadow, or texture (Figure SK1.4). (Color is not covered in this text.)

Sketching as a technique is taught through exercises that improve the ability to "see" while practicing and improving hand/eye coordination.

For the designer, the primary benefit of sketching skills is truly realized in the schematic or preliminary phase of the design process. This includes conceptual/doodle diagrams and image drawings. At this point, fast, loose, sketch-style drawings are a real time saver.

Sketching as a technique has no media restrictions; you can use whatever works or is at hand. However, a variety of pencils, pens, and felt-tip pens are the most popular tools today.

Figure SK1.1

LOOSE SKETCH, LINE ONLY; DETAIL FROM ITALY SKETCH-BOOK

Figure SK1.2

TIGHT SKETCH, FLORIDA STATE UNIVERSITY, DISTANCE LEARNING RECEPTION AREA; ORIGINAL IS 8 × 10.

Figure SK1.4
**COMBINATION OF LINE,
TONE/SHADOW, AND
TEXTURE, FROM ITALY
SKETCHBOOK**

Figure SK1.5

**THUMBNAIL SKETCHES, ¹/₂ × ³/₄ INCHES, LESS THAN
3 MINUTES EACH**

ANNUAL REPORT of the
DIVISION
of BANKING

Gerald Lewis, Comptroller
STATE of FLORIDA
1980

You should keep a sketchbook with you at all times because design ideas can come to you in any place and at any time. In fact, I keep one at my bedside in case I wake up with or even dream up a good idea. A good designer's creative process never sleeps. Since it is impossible to remember all of your ideas during a busy day, putting them on paper is a safe way to prevent you from losing a potentially great one. The sizes and types of sketchbooks vary greatly. Choose one that works for you and that you will actually use.

When you are practicing sketching, draw things that already exist and that you can clearly see, rather than using your imagination. Select things you want to improve on and work and concentrate on them exclusively.

Sketches are pieces of information; they don't have to be considered works of art. They have their own innate beauty and should not be compared with more time-consuming types of drawing.

Often, sketches have a level of simplicity that allows the viewer's eye to finish the picture. This type of sketch is referred to as a vignette *and can save a lot of rendering time.*

Sketching is clearly a very valuable design tool, well worth developing. It can be done in any place and at any time with a minimum amount of equipment and can be used throughout your design career. Often, a thumbnail sketch drawn in a matter of minutes can actually be very representative of what the final drawing or design turns out to be (see Figures SK1.5 and SK1.6). Quick sketches done right in front of the client are one of the most helpful means of getting a point across. Once this valuable skill is learned, it becomes part of your design drawing vocabulary.

THE BASICS

1

What materials do I need?

Basic texts often spend much time and effort in listing and visually illustrating presentation tools and materials, even going so far as to carefully render a mundane drawing pencil. Since even a brief foray through a good art supply store will provide access to all your needs, I simply offer the following as a place to start.

Figure 1.1
PENCIL SKETCH

DRAWING TOOLS

Pencils

A pencil is one of the most versatile tools and is often ignored. The typical drawing pencil is a nonmechanical wood and graphite tool without an eraser. Mechanical, adjustable lead pencils can be used, but the type of lead they use cannot be chiseled. The lead is generally brittle and breaks easily. Keeping a proper point on a pencil is essential to good sketch quality, so keep a pencil sharpener handy or carry a small portable one with you. A chiseled point opens the range of line quality that can be achieved by simply turning the pencil point. The chisel point is achieved by rubbing a sharpened pencil point against a sandpaper block or even just a piece of paper.

As mentioned earlier, the typical drawing pencil does not have an eraser. There is a specific reason for this, and it may be more psychological than actual. The rationale is that because a sketch is a fast, personal expression of an idea or a method of recording what you see, you do not need to fix or correct it, thus eliminating the need for an eraser.

Pencils come in a variety of lead weights, the hardest being 6H and the softest B6. The softer leads are more suitable to sketching while the harder ones are more appropriate for drafting.

Black Felt-, Fiber-, or Nylon-Tip Pens

These are very popular sketching tools and have for the most part replaced all forms of refillable technical ink pens. Many of the drawings in this book were drawn with Pilot, Pentel, and Sanford brands of pens.

These pens come in a variety of points from micro-fine to broad-tip. The basic broad-tip marker is now offered with several point sizes on the same tool. This is meant to make changes in line simpler to accomplish, although the basic chisel-shaped broad-tip is extremely versatile when used sensitively. Versatility is extremely important since we must consider consistency, weight, and character of lines as they affect all of our drawings.

Design Markers

The design marker is a fast, economical, and easy-to-maintain medium. I have been rendering with design markers for more than 30 years, and they have remained effectively the same with some minor variation in the container and variety of tips. These tips vary from fine to broad with some markers offering two or more choices on the same marker. It is my contention that the basic broad-tip marker is by far the most versatile and easy to use. Effective use of markers often depends on some simple choices, such as the paper you use. If the paper was designed for marker use, it often absorbs the marker and causes bleeding, a hard to control effect. Following are some suggestions for the use of markers:

LINE. With the broad-tip marker, turn to the narrow edge for the finest line, the medium edge for mid-range stroke, and the broad side for broadest stroke (see Figure 1.2). For finer lines, I still prefer the basic felt-tip pen but few tools offer the flexibility and versatility of the standard design marker. All brand name markers all basically the same. I make my selection based on color range and comfort of the form of the marker.

Figure 1.2
MARKER LINE WEIGHT EXAMPLES AND VARIATION

TONE/SHADOW. *The design marker is especially effective for defining form and space with tone and shadow using the fast sketch technique. Broad areas of a sketch or the final level in a drawing can be covered in a very short time. Here again we find certain marker characteristics that can be particularly frustrating for the beginner. For example, when covering a plane with vertical or horizontal strokes that are not perfectly aligned, you get a linear effect from the overlapping strokes (Figure 1.3). However, when the effect is controlled it can enhance the vertical movement on a vanishing plane. In addition, overlapping the marker stroke in the same or opposite direction will allow you to get several different values from the same marker. To achieve a wash, or more even effect, you move the marker stroke in a circular motion (Figure 1.4). Different markers are sold that allow you to render in the standard value scale of 0 to 10. Usually, working on white paper provides the 0 value with 10 being black.*

Figure 1.3

MARKER STROKE EFFECTS CAN BE USED TO MOVE A VANISHING PLANE

It is critical to remember that markers are a light to dark medium. *Lay on the lighter values first and build up. For example, if you put a 7 value on paper you cannot bring it back to a lower value with this medium. If you choose to mix media, such as markers and colored pencils, some lightening of value can be achieved (see Figure 1.5).*

TEXTURE/MATERIALS. *By using the different edges of the marker and different strokes, you can create a variety of textures. If you are at a drafting board, the T-square and triangle can help control your strokes while not creating too tight an effect in the drawing.*

In this book we are only concerned with warm and cool values of gray and the role they play in monochromatic studies and drawings. Obviously, markers come in a complete range of colors that continue to make this medium one of the most popular for designers in both sketching and final-level drawings for client-oriented presentation.

Figure 1.4

MARKER STROKE IN CIRCULAR MANNER GIVES A SMOOTHER EFFECT; AVOID OVERLAPS

Figure 1.5

LOOSE MARKER STUDY ON YELLOW TRACING PAPER

Figure 1.6

BASIC TOOLS—PENCIL, FELT-TIP, AND DESIGN MARKER—AND THEIR USES

MISCELLANEOUS. *For sketching or rendering, any tool at hand or whatever works for you is acceptable (Figure 1.6). Some other popular choices are colored pencils, pastels, chalks, inks, and even the old standard ballpoint pen (Figure 1.7).*

Sketch exercises often include the use of found objects to encourage the student to loosen up by breaking away from the standard tools. For example, you can use tree twigs, Q-tips, or burnt wood matches which may be dipped in colored water or inks.

SKETCHING

Figure 1.7
SKETCH DONE WITH BLUE BALL POINT

DRAWING PAPER

The Sketchbook

Choosing a sketchbook is very simple since the media they are suitable for is usually described on the cover.

The key to getting the right effect from your paper is its tooth—*the coarseness or smoothness of the surface. Any good-quality, medium-tooth paper will work with pencil. It allows you to develop rich values and textures. The coarser papers are more absorbent and may cause felt tips or markers to* bleed, *a frustrating and often negative factor in controlling the media in a drawing.*

So usually it is simply the size that determines the selection of a sketchbook, based on ease of use rather than the paper, which tends to be relatively standard.

Tracing Paper

There are three basic types of tracing paper: parchment (mentioned previously), vellum, and graphics paper. The latter two are high-quality papers suitable for a variety of media and are durable enough for commercial reproduction. Tracing paper, as we will see later on in this text, is a crucial element in the overlay *method.*

YELLOW OR WHITE PARCHMENT TRACING PAPER.
This is the least expensive tracing paper and comes in rolls or pads of varying widths and sizes. The paper is very fragile and is suitable only for preliminary types of sketches and studies. It is meant to be used, abused, and inevitably thrown away. Designers often refer to it as trash *or* bumwad. *Psychologically, this paper is seen as a preliminary medium for fast, loose drawings that are clearly subject to change. Soft pencils and felt-tip pens are ideal on this surface since anything harder will easily tear the paper.*

VELLUM AND GRAPHICS PAPER. *Generally, vellum is recommended for drafting while graphics paper is used for presentation purposes. Graphics paper is a good surface for graphite, inks, and markers. Drawings on vellum and graphics paper can be saved as originals using a*

variety of reproduction methods or used in final presentations when mounted properly.

Miscellaneous Papers

A tremendous selection of drawing papers may be bought by the sheet. I suggest once again visiting the art supply store to see and sample them.

BASIC DRAWING ADVICE

The very first step to success in drawing is to loosen up. Drawing, like many athletic activities, is a connection between mind, eye, and hand. Thus, as with all physical activity or exercise, a warm-up phase is suggested. Simple movement of the arms, wrists, and fingers can be effective. When drawing, having tight muscles and joints will have an adverse effect, so remember to be loose, free, and relaxed. This will allow you to enjoy and enhance your drawing experience.

LINE

2

What is line?

Line is the basic element common to all drawings. To the beginner, just making the first mark that destroys the purity and perfection of the white sheet of paper can certainly instill fear. Remember that this fear is irrational, so be bold and draw away!

In the sketching phase, making lines with mechanical tools, a T-square, and a triangle is not allowed.

A beginner who does not feel he or she is artistic, often exclaims, "I can't even draw a straight line!" We deal with this by stressing that design drawing and sketching can be learned. In fact, in freehand drawing it is the acceptance of the illusion that the line is straight that really counts. Of course, with enough practice you can achieve relatively straight lines by improving your hand/eye coordination. In the final analysis, the ability to draw a line from point A to point B (Figure 2.1) does not an artist make!

Figure 2.1

DRAW A STRAIGHT LINE IN ONE STROKE

Figure 2.2
DON'T SHAKE OUT THE LINE

When attempting to draw a straight line, rest your hand firmly on a steady surface and move only your hand and forearm across the paper. Avoid what I refer to as shaking out *the line (Figure 2.2). Try to draw the line with one bold, confident stroke, rather than stopping and starting to correct for direction. An architectural effect can be achieved by overlapping the line at the corners of a shape or form (Figure 2.3).

Figure 2.3
EXAMPLE OF "ARCHITECTURAL" CORNER OVERLAP

ELEMENTS OF A LINE

The three basic elements of a line are consistency, line weight variation, and quality.

Consistency

Practice this effect in a drawing by keeping the lines the same weight (thickness) or character no matter what the subject (Figure 2.4). This is an interesting but limited technique that is more of an exercise of control. It is often used more effectively in technical or mechanical drawing.

Figure 2.4
LINE CONSISTENCY

SKETCHING

Figure 2.5
LINE WEIGHT VARIATION

Weight Variation

Visually, this is the thickness of a line. The thinner the line, the lighter the weight. These weight differences help us to distinguish between architectural elements and to define individual forms (Figure 2.5). Light-weight lines usually are internal and help to complete the form. Medium-weight or profile lines define the form and help place it spatially. Heavy-weight lines define architectural features or act as base plane lines that help to ground the form. The two sketches in Figure 2.7 show line weight variation, with white trace.

Quality (Character)

Quality is the most expressive use of line and it truly enhances a sketch style. Good line quality helps define and make the illusion of curved or round shapes or forms more believable (Figure 2.6). Most often, however, the quality of line is best utilized in freeform objects such as plants, clothing, window coverings, and many other elements typically found in residential or commercial interior or exterior sketches.

Figure 2.6
LINE QUALITY

21   LINE

Figure 2.7

SKETCHES WITH LINE WEIGHT VARIATION ON WHITE TRACING PAPER, 11 × 14 INCHES

What is light?

Light is the element of design that defines all that we see and how we see it. Sunlight and artificial light from any man-made source are the primary choices we have to determine how our drawings read and make a visual impact. We distinguish shapes or forms in space through tone, value, or shade *(basically interchangeable terms)* and shadow.

TONE, VALUE, OR SHADE

The terms tone, value, *and* shade *refer to the way light affects a shape, object, or form.* Value *is most often used to grade lightness or darkness. Values range from zero (0), which equals white, to 10, which equals black.*

A value of 10 is usually reserved for shadow based on the rule of thumb, "Shadow is darker than shade." This is an important factor because we can only clearly read form relationships with a lighter value next to a darker one. A value of 10 on a form with shadow value of 10 would blend together and the clarity of the form would be lost (Figure 3.1).

Changes in value are produced by altering the direction and intensity of the light source.

SHADOW

There are an almost unlimited number of formulas for casting shadows. The key to understanding the use of shadow in a drawing is to follow the rule, "What you see is what you get." It is no more complicated than that. Reality-based shadows can be created using a simple lamp as a source on objects or models to simulate the scene you want to create.

Shadows often have an umber, *a darker aura, and* penumbra, *a lighter aura. Shadows may appear crisp with hard edges or soft and blend more into the drawing. Your drawings should always maintain a clear and consistent light source.*

People who view your drawings may not be artistic, but they are used to seeing the effects of light in their daily lives. So, if you want them to accept the illusion of what you have drawn, your use of light will be critical.

ONE-POINT SHADOW CASTING

1. Select a light source.

2. Apply tone to the form.

3. Select points on the planes of the form that will block light and cast a shadow.

4. Draw consistent angles from these points (typically 30 degrees).

5. From the top shadow casting points, use 45-degree angle lines to determine the length of the shadow. In reality, the shadow changes as the angle of the light source changes. When a light source is directly over an object, it produces no shadow.

6. The 45-degree lines will intersect the 30-degree lines then close out the shadow with a parallel line and a line to the vanishing point (VP).

7. The same principles apply to this open-leg table.

TWO-POINT SHADOW CASTING

1. Select a light source.

2. Draw lines through the shadow casting points in the direction the shadow will fall.

3. Draw a line parallel to the object at point A.

4. Where this line intersects a shadow casting line from the light source, draw a line toward vanishing point left (VPL).

5. Where this line intersects the other shadow casting line from the light source, draw a line toward vanishing point right (VPR).

6. Close the shadow with a parallel line back to point B.

Figure 3.2 shows a shadow cast through a window at a 45-degree angle.

Figure 3.2
**SHADOW CAST THROUGH A
WINDOW, 45° ANGLE**

*Figures 3.3 through 3.8 are sketches done in various
media and with different types of light.*

Figure 3.3
**SKETCH WITH LIGHT DONE
WITH A SANFORD SHARPIE
ULTRAFINE PEN**

Figure 3.4

**SKETCH DONE WITH A
BLACK UNIBALL MICRO PEN**

Figure 3.5

**SKETCH DONE WITH
A BLACK UNIBALL MICRO PEN**

Figure 3.6

**SKETCH DONE WITH A
#3 PENCIL**

Figure 3.7

**SKETCH WITH NATURAL
SUN LIGHT**

Figure 3.8

**BOLD SHADOW, NATURAL
LIGHT**

SKETCHING

TEXTURE

What is texture?

Texture is the element of design that helps define the character of a space. Everything has texture ranging from rough to smooth. The type and extent of texture you use also affect the principle of design: emphasis. Seize the opportunity to express texture since it produces the most interesting, active, sensual, tactile character in the drawing.

MATERIALS

Both natural and man-made materials are affected by textures and patterns. In exterior sketches we find plant life, water, stone, and a variety of other natural materials. If there are architectural features in the drawing, both natural and man-made materials will come into play. When sketching interior spaces we find wood, stone, brick, glass, wall covering, floor covering, and fabric as popular materials (Figure 4.1).

Obviously, certain materials are much easier to draw than others. It pays to emphasize those, while merely suggesting others (Figure 4.2). One of the keys to drawing materials is to carefully study and understand them. For example, there are certain distinct grain patterns in trees that are grown and harvested for furniture. The patterns

Figure 4.1
TEXTURE STUDY, BOLD CONTRAST

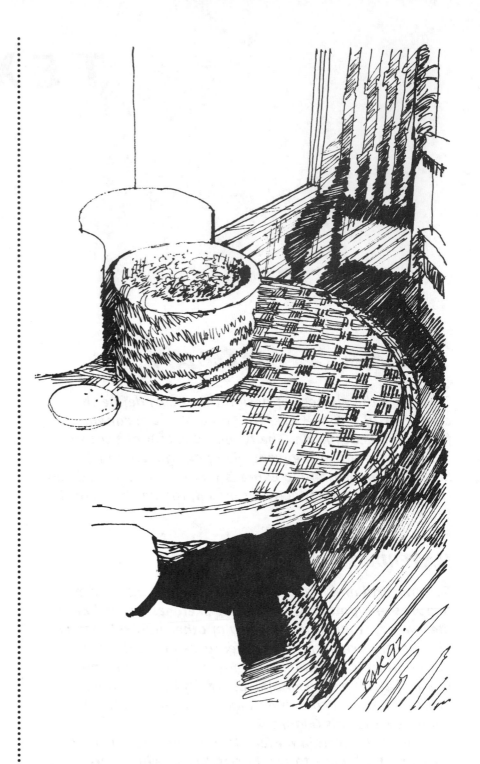

vary in the way the tree is cut and whether hardwood or veneer is used. As mentioned previously, the average person may not be artistic but he or she has a sense of real-

Figure 4.2
WOOD GRAIN STUDY

ity. If your drawings do not reflect this quality, the viewer will not accept your illusion.

The way stone, brick, and tile are laid also creates identifiable characteristics. These may be especially apparent with materials that have standard sizes. The most popular flooring material is carpet which is an excellent source of textural treatment. Again you must take care in how you draw carpet since it is a milled product that produces a clear nonrandom linear quality. To keep the floor from appearing to fly up, both pattern and carpet pile must diminish in size in a perspective sketch.

Whether it is a window or part of a piece of furniture, glass is often a difficult material to draw. Changing of the value or clarity of what you see in the room from what you see outside helps the viewer believe the material must be glass. This would also be true of drawing what you see through a glass tabletop (Figure 4.3). It is important to use techniques triggering cues and symbols that make it

Figure 4.3
TEXTURE STUDY WITH GLASS

impossible for the viewers not to believe what you want them to see.

Wall coverings and fabrics are materials that can be used to enhance a drawing. Often it is the pattern that brings the material to life. Drawing at a small scale, it is impossible to clearly see all of the detail of a pattern. Simply suggesting the pattern with a convincing use of texture and line will be effective. Basic materials, such as nylon and leather, can be more easily suggested by clearly defining the way the material is used on the furniture—the tufting, the seams, and the skirt, for instance.

Textures and materials may be drawn generically or realistically. There are several types of generic textures: stippling (the use of graded dots, Figure 4.4), cross-hatching, loops, and so on. It is important not to use the same generic texture for different materials in the same draw-

Figure 4.4

**TEXTURE STUDY WITH
GENERIC STIPPLING**

ing. If you use stippling for hard-surface materials such as plaster or concrete, you must not use it for a soft fabric. This would only confuse the viewer who is adjusting his or her eye to the use of your generic texture.

Although realistically capturing the illusion of a specific material on paper often depends on your drawing skills, you must have a working knowledge of its growth patterns, structural characteristics, construction, and basic features or details. With patience and practice, the proper emphasis on textures, materials, and patterns in your drawings will prove to be a source of satisfaction and pleasure while enriching the visual effect through a strong tactile experience.

E N T O U R A G E

5

What is entourage?

Entourage refers to all the elements in a drawing that humanize it or bring it to life. In fact, several books on the market today are exclusively dedicated to entourage as a tool for the drawing student to copy or use as a tracing file. The books predominantly show figures in a variety of scales and poses, as well as plants, trees, cars, and miscellaneous elements found in exterior and interior drawings. These books have their place in drawing education, but you should avoid using them as a crutch to replace practicing and learning to draw the things they offer.

THE HUMAN FIGURE

The human figure should play an essential and vital role in sketching, design drawing, and final presentation perspectives. The style and type of figure may vary depending on the purpose of the drawing.

The best way to learn to draw the human figure is to use real-life models (see Chapter 6). To develop an understanding of the human figure, you can learn a lot by simply studying some basic anatomy. I tell students who feel the human figure is just too difficult to learn to draw that if they can learn to draw a complex piece of furniture by looking at it carefully and observing its form and details, they can learn to draw a human figure with practice.

In design drawing it is essential to use figures to establish scale and proportion. There are several typical styles that meet out information needs.

Even at relatively small scale, the quick-sketch-style figure can be very effective in displaying the anthropo-metric relationships involved in your design solutions (Figure 5.1). People tend to relate everything in their environment to themselves, which makes the use of the human figure even more important.

TREES AND PLANTS

Trees and plants in exterior drawings are an excellent source of free-form lines and texture. They react strongly to natural light, creating strong shadow patterns. Once again, drawing on site and practicing what you see is vital. Studying growth patterns and leaf shapes makes these elements much more believable in your drawings.

Plants also play a role in most interiors. Learn the most typical varieties of indoor plants and practice draw-

Figure 5.1
FIGURE SCALE EXAMPLE

Figure 5.2
GENERIC PLANTS

SKETCHING

ing them. Ficus trees, cornplants, ferns, palms, and a variety of ivies are just a few examples.

In sketching there are several generic leaf and plant types that can be used effectively once you understand plant forms and can make them look convincing (Figures 5.2 and 5.3).

STUFF FOR SKETCHING

Stuff *refers to everything else one finds in common exteriors and interiors that makes them look like someone lives or works there (Figure 5.4). Stuff shows that the spaces drawn are a real part of the daily environment. In exteriors we find such things as cars, buses, signs, lamp posts, and fences. In interiors we find books, telephones, magazines, glass and tableware, and, most important, artwork. Paintings, wall art of all types, and sculpture often add real strength and credibility to the designed space. This list of stuff goes on and on but, as you can clearly see, anything that can be utilized to humanize the spaces we design gives the feeling that these spaces really exist. The*

Figure 5.3
GENERIC LEAF EXAMPLES

Figure 5.4

STUFF EXAMPLES—THINGS THAT BRING A DRAWING TO LIFE

Figure 5.5

STUFF WITH TEXTURE

things we choose to study, whether they are interior or exterior, comprise a still life. You must compose the drawing the same way a photographer or artist would, while continuing to concentrate on line, tone/shadow, and texture/materials (Figure 5.5).

The proper use of entourage as illustrated in the three sections of this book is one of the most important parts of drawing for design and the client communication process. In the final analysis, human beings are our clients and the source of our livelihood; they are who we design for. So the humanization of our drawings, first practiced in sketch format, is not merely a source of drawing pleasure for us but is critical to the client recognition factor and to achieving success in our role as a designer.

SKETCH EXERCISES

6

How do I loosen up?

The most informal of the "loosen-up" exercises involves the use of line in a variety of movements across the page (Figure 6.1). These exercises should be fast paced and serve only as a warm up.

As discussed in Chapter 2, the most important elements of line are consistency, weight variation, *and* quality (character).

Obviously, all lines in sketch exercises must be free-hand without the aid of mechanical tools. Basic line exercises may be done in the sketchbook and may be controlled by the size of the space they are done in, typically squares or rectangles: 1" × 2", 1½" × 1½", or 2" × 2".

1. BASIC LINE CONSISTENCY

Use a variety of vertical, horizontal, and diagonal line directions or vary the spacing while keeping the line a consistent thickness (Figure 6.2). Control is the key to this exercise.

Figure 6.1

"LOOSEN UP" LINE

2. LINE CONSISTENCY WITH VARIETY

Use your imagination to draw loops, swirls, or any other interesting line movements (Figure 6.3). Or draw lines with character in a perspective or receding effect (Figure 6.4).

Figure 6.2

LINE STUDY EXERCISE

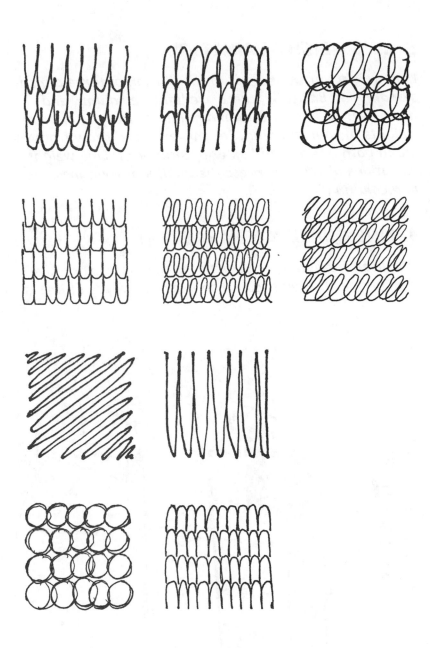

Figure 6.3
LINE STUDIES WITH LOOPS

Figure 6.4

**LINES WITH CHARACTER
SHOWING RECEDING EFFECT**

41 SKETCH EXERCISES

3. LINE WEIGHT VARIATION

Line weight variation adds to the illusion of three-dimensional form. Basically, there are light-, medium-, and heavy-weight lines. Use a minimum of three distinct line weights in your drawing. For this exercise, draw from real life in both interior and exterior situations. Line weight variations also can express the quality of roundness, as in a column (Figure 6.5).

4. LINE QUALITY (CHARACTER)

Line used for quality (character) is the most expressive type of line. The most common use of this type of line is

Figure 6.5

LINE WEIGHT USED TO CREATE ILLUSION OF ROUNDNESS

found in free-form or organic shapes and forms, either natural or man-made.

In nature trees and plants provide interesting growth patterns and leaf shapes. Many other features such as grass and groundcover offer excellent possibilities for the use of line quality.

Architectural elements including roof materials, wall facing materials, and a variety of other features in building styles let us use line to develop their character.

Interiors have a wealth of subjects for our line quality exercises. Draperies, loose fabric, throw pillows, interior plants, and art are just a few examples.

The following exercises give you an excellent opportunity to practice the three elements of line: consistency, weight variation, and quality (character).

5. EXTERIOR SKETCH

Exterior sketching is an excellent way to practice hand/eye coordination while enjoying the outdoors and natural surroundings. You can sketch things you want to record for future reference. This may be the architectural elements and features of places you visit, or you can sketch in nature just for the sheer pleasure of doing it.

Whether sketching natural or man-made elements, it is important to remember the basics: line, tone/shadow, and texture/materials.

When sketching trees and plants, look carefully— "learn to see"—at their form, growth patterns, shapes, and textures. Natural sunlight is the strongest source of light and will strongly affect the elements and the impact of your drawing. Sunny days usually produce the shadows that make the boldest sketches.

Select your subject matter carefully and with the eye of a camera compose your sketchbook page. Composition remains a consideration whether you are drawing a major landscape or city scape, a single element, or even the smallest detail.

As a beginner you should limit the scope of what you choose to draw and keep track of the time it takes you to accomplish what you set out to achieve. Over time, with

Figure 6.6

BUILDING STUDY SKETCH, LINE ONLY, 10 MINUTES—CAPITOL BUILDING, TALLAHASSEE

SKETCHING   **44**

practice, you will be able to increase the pace and shorten the time it takes to do these sketches. Your knowledge of basic one-point and two-point perspective is important. While drawing outdoors, look for and identify the ground line, horizon line, and vanishing points and establish a picture plane that will increase the illusion of a believable perspective view. The two sketches in Figure 6.7 are exterior details.

Always note the goals you wish to achieve in your sketch exercises; this allows you to measure your success. For example, I will study a building's form using line only. Or I will study the leaf growth pattern of a particular tree.

Set time limits for these sketches from a few minutes to an hour.

6. INTERIOR SKETCH

Interior sketch subjects are always available and are not controlled by weather conditions. You can study whole rooms in residential and nonresidential situations. You can study furniture relationships; usually a grouping of

Figure 6.7

EXTERIOR DETAIL, 5 MINUTES, FROM ITALY SKETCHBOOK

three objects works well (Figure 6.8). You can study any interior detail.

You can actually set up a still life to practice drawing specific items that express the shapes, forms, and textures that will offer a challenge (See, for example, Figures 4.3 and 5.4). Or go out and look for things that are interesting to practice on.

Figure 6.8

INTERIOR ITALIAN DETAILS, 3 TO 5 MINUTES

Figure 6.9
INTERIOR ITALIAN DETAILS, 3 TO 5 MINUTES

Figure 6.10
INTERIOR ITALIAN DETAILS, 3 TO 5 MINUTES

7. FIGURE STUDY

Gesture Drawings

Gesture drawings are an excellent beginning figure exercise. They help you "learn to see" and give you the chance to "loosen up." In the classroom you can use other students as models; at home, use friends or family members.

The time for this exercise should be from 30 to 90 seconds. The goal is to capture the gesture of the pose, the forces of movement, and the sense of equilibrium. The pace is fast, so use a soft lead pencil or a felt-tip pen; don't outline the figure but use bold lines and a sense of mass.

Since 30 seconds is a very short time, your model can hold almost any active pose. In fact, some of the best models are students who have studied ballet or karate. Two models posing together may make for some interesting results.

In the gesture drawing, human form or clothing details are simply not important; there is just not enough time to cover those elements (Figure 6.11).

8. FIGURE STUDY

Changing the time of the pose to $1\frac{1}{2}$, 3, and 10 minutes, for example, allows you to see how much can be accomplished in short time-span jumps. The shorter time spans still maintain gesture quality while allowing for some observation of human form and clothing (Figures 6.12 and 6.13). At 10 minutes you can concentrate on more detail and more expressive line quality (character). Of course, the type of pose changes with the length of time and becomes simpler in the complexity of human movement. These studies increase your ability to "learn to see" and your hand/eye coordination, while supporting the importance of the figure in the drawing process for communication.

Figure 6.11

**GESTURE DRAWINGS, 30 SEC-
ONDS**

SKETCHING   **50**

Figure 6.12
**GESTURE DRAWING,
90 SECONDS**

Figure 6.13
FIGURE STUDY, 5 MINUTES

9. STILL LIFE STUDY

These studies may be a single object or a complex composition. In the classroom, a good variety of shapes, forms, and textures work best. They may include cans, bottles, purses, jackets, drafting tools, plants, and various found objects. Still lifes improve hand/eye coordination.

No Lift

No lift is one of the two most popular hand/eye coordination exercises.

Look at the subject and start drawing anywhere without lifting your sketch tool off the paper. Use line only; you may alter the pressure to change line weight, but in this exercise you are not concerned with tone/shadow or texture (Figure 6.14).

Draw the line relatively slowly. You are not working at the speed of a gesture drawing so you have more control.

Although this drawing will never be literal, your accuracy will improve with practice. The average time allotted to this drawing is from 1 to 5 minutes.

No Look

No look is the second most popular and most challenging hand/eye coordination exercise. It requires great patience and self-control; even the best renderers are frustrated by it.

Look at the subject and start anywhere, but don't look at your drawing at any time. The pace is slow, but be confident and do not worry about accuracy.

You can lift your drawing tool from the paper, but since you can't look you will probably lose your place and not regain it. If you look at the drawing at any time during the exercise, the exercise is over.

Time for this exercise is usually 1 to 5 minutes.

Again, you are only using line and are not concerned with tone/shadow and texture (Figure 6.15). Practice this technique in the classroom or at home, and if the results are even close to resembling reality, you have done quite well.

Figure 6.14
"NO LIFT" EXAMPLES

no lift

don't lift

Figure 6.15
"NO LOOK" EXAMPLE

10. TONE/SHADOW

Tone/shadow exercises can be done in either interior or exterior locations. In the classroom specifically, setting up a still life works well. A good source of light is very important.

Study the subject for tone and shadow only (Figure 6.16). Don't outline objects, but use tone to define form and shadow to reinforce the direction and quantity of light. Remember the rule of thumb, "Shadow is darker than shade." Do not consider texture or pattern.

Figure 6.16
EXAMPLE SHOWING TONE ONLY

Time can vary for this exercise, depending on the subject, but you will need a minimum of 3 minutes.

This exercise helps you learn to better react to forms in space and will play a vital role in the overlay *method.*

11. TEXTURE/MATERIALS

The first exercise in texture/materials is a simple controlled "learn to see" study.

Look at specific textures or materials and draw them in a square or rectangle (Figure 6.19). Or just have fun playing with texture (Figure 6.18).

The second exercise can be done in both interior and exterior locations.

In the classroom, use the same still life for all of these exercises. The still life must include objects that have clearly definable textures or patterns. Wood, glass, coarse fabrics, and plants are just some things that work well. Everything has texture, but things with smooth or slick textures don't work as well. You can, however, feel free to use some generic textures such as stippling or cross-hatching.

Figure 6.17
**EXAMPLE SHOWING TEXTURE
ONLY**

Study texture and materials only; you must disregard line and light (Figure 6.17). It is not necessary to draw the whole still life; be selective within the time limit.

Time is again relative but a minimum of 10 minutes is effective.

Figure 6.18

TEXTURE EXERCISE, LOOSE

Figure 6.19
TEXTURE EXERCISE, REAL AND GENERIC

Figure 6.20

EXAMPLE USING TONE AND TEXTURE

12. LINE, TONE/SHADOW, AND TEXTURE/MATERIAL

This exercise is usually the final step after undertaking the previous two exercises. Having studied the still life for light and texture/material (pattern) separately, you now put them together selectively with line effects to produce the strongest drawing (Figure 6.20). As you will see later on in the book, this is the basic concept behind the over-lay method.

Once again the time spent is relative to the scope and complexity of the still life.

These are only a sampling of the many exercises available to you as a drawing student, but they are an excellent start and source for a concerted effort to practice the skill of hand/eye coordination. Practice is the key to reinforcing ability and building confidence, and your confidence will show in even better sketches.

Figure 6.21

REDUNDANT LINE

This is a good time to define what I call the *redundant line*. It ties into what I call the *coloring book effect*. When you produce a fully outlined drawing and color it in, maybe even try as a kid to stay inside the lines, this gives the *coloring book effect*. This is not always the most interesting, subtle, or expressive way to draw. In fact, using two tones to define a form is sometimes more effective and it removes the need for a line at that place. I call the line that can be successfully removed the redundant line.

Section Two

DESIGN DRAWING

What is design drawing?

Design drawing *is a visual language or shorthand used in the schematic or preliminary phase of the design process to help in the search for potential solutions to design problems.*

In this section we will examine conceptual/doodle diagrams and various types of perspective drawings that are used for design drawing. These types of drawings are meant to be used in house by the designer while problem solving and are generally not shown to the client. This type of drawing has its own look, style, and integrity, and it should not be judged on rendering skill or artistic merit. In fact, it is the speed with which this style of drawing can be put on paper, not the accuracy, that counts.

In certain high-stress situations, these quick drawing skills can be essential. At the student level, whether they are short-term sketch problems or eight-hour sketch problems, these skills may be a deciding factor in examinations for professional licensing.

In certain situations, however, design drawing can be used to create a quick sketch to effectively express an idea to a client. One typical example popularized over the years is referred to as napkin art, *so called because a designer sketches an idea on a napkin during a business lunch. This skill impresses most clients and often reinforces the historic phrase, "A picture is worth a thousand words." Most graphic educators consider design drawing to be the most valuable and lasting tool students carry with them into the design profession.*

61

Figure SK2.1

open to lake

Figure SK2.2

Figure SK2.3

CONCEPTUAL/ DOODLE DIAGRAMS

7

What is a conceptual/doodle diagram?

The conceptual/doodle diagram is the heart of the schematic phase of design. It is the designer's first marks on paper after research and programming have taken place. Conceptual/doodles are the designer's visual shorthand using drawings that are sketchlike, small, and fast. They allow the designer to examine many different ideas at this preliminary stage of the design process. Conceptual/doodle diagrams are in-house aids to the designer and, as a general rule, they are not shown to the client. This means they only need to be understood by the designer and are not necessarily a communication tool.

Everyone has doodled at one time or another and it can be a satisfying, if mindless, activity. In our definition, we have added the word conceptual in front of doodle to remind us that this activity is definitely not meant to be mindless. Figures 7.1(a) and (b) are not conceptual/doodle diagrams.

Figure 7.1

EXAMPLES OF WHAT IS NOT A CONCEPTUAL/DOODLE DIAGRAM

Conceptual/doodle *is defined as a form of design graphics expressing a word, space, or action, to be used to examine potential design solutions in the schematic phase of the design process. The key word is* potential *since at this time you should look at alternatives that may be further developed (Figures 7.2 and 7.3).*

Figure 7.2

CONCEPTUAL/DOODLE DIAGRAMS—MOVABLE CLOTHES STORAGE

Figure 7.3

**CONCEPTUAL/DOODLE
DIAGRAM WITH SECTION
AND SCALE EXAMPLES**

Diagram *is defined as an involved series of conceptual/doodles. If a conceptual/doodle is a shorthand word, then a diagram is a sentence or even a paragraph. From a design standpoint, a lone conceptual/doodle is usually meaningless if it is not part of a diagram.*

As designers, conceptual/doodle diagrams become our own personal shorthand. They may be realistic, symbolic, *or* abstract.

The vast majority of conceptual/doodle diagrams are symbolic, since realistic drawings tend to be more time consuming. If they are repeated often enough, abstract drawings that have meaning for us eventually become symbolic. For example, if there were one place left on earth where Coca-Cola was not sold, its symbol would be abstract to those people. However, if by some form of magic a Coke machine were installed, the abstract letters would, in a very short span of time, become symbolic of the cold soft drink they represent.

CONCEPTUAL/
DOODLE
DIAGRAMS

The basic design process starts with data collection and programming, identifying client needs and clarifying their image and character (Figure 7.4). You begin the pre-liminary design process with conceptual/doodle diagrams using the *elements* and *principles* of design. The following

Figure 7.4

DIAGRAMS FOR A PLAY SPACE FOR CHILDREN WITH DISABILITIES

are typical elements: *form, scale, color, texture, and light. The* principles *are: unity, variety, harmony, balance, emphasis, repetition, and proportion.*

When working on preliminary designs, I recommend moving from the macrocosm, or overview, to the micro-cosm, or smallest detail (Figure 7.5). When first working with conceptual/doodle diagrams, beginning design stu-dents are tempted to jump to preconceived notions for design solutions rather than letting them develop through the natural course of design evolution. They often have the tendency to work backwards by coming up with a

Figure 7.5

STUDY FROM MACROCOSM TO MICROCOSM—BEACH HOUSE EXAMPLE

HOUSE

SITE

CASE

INTERIOR

CONCEPTUAL/ DOODLE DIAGRAMS

69

Figure 7.6

EXAMPLE OF A SCALE FIGURE TYPE FOR USE IN DIAGRAMS

design decision and then doing conceptual/doodle diagrams to support the end result. This, of course, entirely defeats the purpose of the diagram. The use of conceptual/doodle diagrams is not only critical in the design development phase but will serve as proof of a logically conceived and functional preliminary design solution.

Reminder: At this point it is evident that sketch figures are very important in conceptual/doodle diagrams to help establish a sense of scale and proportion (Figure 7.6).

BUBBLE FLOW DIAGRAMS

Bubble flow diagrams are one of the most popular schematic phases of design studies. They are used for space planning and circulation. A five-step bubble flow version that stylistically falls under the umbrella of conceptual/doodle diagrams leads to a preliminary floor plan.

An unlimited number of bubble flow diagrams may be generated by client information in the facilities program statement. Of course, the number of diagrams the designer pursues will be controlled by contract deadlines—time limitations are always a factor. The bubble flow diagram with the best potential will be developed in the final design phase. As in all conceptual/doodle diagrams the bubbles are a designer's shorthand; they are often accompanied by a specific and, in some cases, lengthy verbal description.

All of the spaces listed in the client's design program should be represented by an individual bubble. It is advisable to place the name of the space or room in the bubble. The bubbles should be drawn free-hand since the use of a circle template is too formal and time consuming.

Following are the definitions for using bubbles as a language:

1. *The size of the bubble relates directly to the size of the space it defines. This is simply based on proportion: a small bubble may represent a 50-square foot space, while a bubble twice its size represents a 100-square-foot area.*

2. *When two bubbles are physically touching this indicates that two spaces are adjacent to one another. But, this step does not clarify what is between the spaces, which may be a wall, partition, or some other form of space divider.*

3. *Overlapping bubbles indicate spaces that interact, share function, or are linked in concept through open-space planning.*

CONCEPTUAL/
DOODLE
DIAGRAMS

4. *When there is an opening between the bubbles, this indicates that the spaces do not touch and may be separated by a corridor.*

EXAMPLE OF A FIVE-STEP BUBBLE FLOW DIAGRAM

Step 1. This step indicates the *WHERE* or location of each space as communicated to the designer and defined by the client's needs.

Step 2. This is a vital step in a circulation study. It indicates *HOW* the people are moved through the spaces. A key with strong graphic symbols should be used to indicate major or minor circulation patterns or any other form of movement including site lines or view.

Step 3. This step converts the bubbles into basic geometric shapes that will become recognizable as a floor plan in Step 4.

Step 4. This step shows a single-line floor plan with recognizable architectural features such as doors, windows, fireplaces, and so on. Spaces that are separated by walls or some other form of divider are now clear.

Step 5. The final step is a preliminary layout. It should be to scale or "eyeball" to scale. All wall thicknesses and architectural features are shown. Floor materials with appropriate textures should be shown. It is beneficial at this point in the schematic phase of design to place generic furniture in the plan. Commitment to specific pieces will be made at a later stage in the design process.

CONCEPTUAL/
DOODLE
DIAGRAMS

At the completion of a five-step bubble flow, you will see a clear progression of thought and analysis. When placing the steps side by side, you not only see their logical relationships but often you are able to spot a problem that might have been missed or inadequately solved. The preliminary floor plan will meet all the client's functional and circulation needs. Now you are ready to start to make all modifications to achieve a final floor plan that will be used for specifications and eventual construction. Of course, this potential design solution is in the second dimension, or plan view only. You must do conceptual/doodle diagrams in elevation, section, and perspective at the same time to truly develop your design in a logical sequence. As a quick sketch-style drawing tool, a five-step bubble flow can play an important role in helping to solve problems in the schematic phase of design development.

PERSPECTIVE DRAWING

8

What is a perspective drawing?

The perspective drawing is one of the oldest and most popular means of design communication. Clients tend to feel more comfortable with this pictorial view, which is often much easier to relate to than the floor plans, elevations, or sections commonly used by designers to express design solutions. Two key buzz words often related to perspective drawing are reality and believability. I teach students not to search for magic solutions or secret formulas but to accept and recognize the "what you see is what you get" concept. Simplistically speaking, we see in a modification of one- and two-point perspective, depending on how we move our head and eyes to view a room or space.

The following terms are basic to the understanding of perspective drawing:

Station point: The point from which a person views a space or object.

Ground line: The place the visual plane meets the ground.

Horizon line: An imaginary line that is always consistent with the eye level.

Vanishing point: *A point or points that are always on the horizon line; the points where parallel lines converge.*

Picture plane: *A plane in space that frames and defines the perspective that is drawn.*

In more than 30 years as a professional renderer, I have found that a clear majority of interior perspectives are best shown in one-point perspective, while the best exterior views seem to be in two-point perspective. You should certainly learn the means to produce mechanical perspectives as part of your foundation study, but you should also learn freehand and eyeball methods as soon as possible. Almost all of my perspective drawings have been done by the eyeball method, with the exception of some complex cases where I used mechanical methodology. Therefore, it seems practical to present only eyeball methods in this book.

There are a wide variety of perspective types and a great diversity of effective drawing styles. Rendering is clearly an art form and must be subject to personal style and taste. It is important to be exposed to many design drawing styles, even emulating those you admire, but after a certain length of time your own style will emerge.

The following types of perspectives will be presented in this chapter:

- *Conceptual doodle/diagram perspectives*
- *Image perspectives*
- *Final perspectives*

These perspective drawing types and the amount of rendering in them relates strictly to the role they play in the design process. Time and budgetary factors will affect their use as well. This is especially true for drawings used in client presentations which are often considered extras and are billed accordingly. If they are eliminated, a potential communication gap may develop that may prove costly at a later date.

CONCEPTUAL DOODLE/DIAGRAM PERSPECTIVES

As defined in Chapter 7, conceptual doodles may be plan, elevation, section, or perspective drawings. The conceptual doodle/diagram perspective is free hand, small, fast, and loose. It may or may not be in color. It is not meant to be pretty, but rather it should express action/reaction, showing a particular potential design solution that is best seen and understood in the third dimension (Figure 8.1). Unlike traditional perspectives, it can have notes, arrows, or other symbols drawn all over it to help the designer in the creative process. Remember, conceptual doodle/ diagrams are part of the preliminary phase of design and are considered in-house drawings that are not used for client presentation. These perspective sketches are most effective when illustrating things in the design that change, move, or have some flexibility—action/reaction.

Figure 8.1a

CONCEPTUAL/DOODLE DIAGRAM PERSPECTIVE ILLUSTRATING ACTION/REACTION

PERSPECTIVE
DRAWING

conceptual/doodle/persp.

IMAGE PERSPECTIVES

The image perspective is a tremendously effective in-house design tool, since all design projects deal with the clients' concept of their own image and character. They should be done in eyeball sketch style and generally are 8½ × 11 inches or smaller in size. These drawings are part of the schematic or preliminary phase of design, so they allow the designer to examine many potential solutions as quickly as possible. Image perspectives relate directly to the use of the elements and principles of design. So the use of line, tone, texture, or color will depend on what the designer is trying to study about the space.

Image perspectives thus become a great source of information concerning form and scale relationships, light sources, texture and material alternatives, and much more. Neatness and accuracy are not a major characteristic of an image perspective; time spent on these drawings should be kept to a minimum, approximately 10 minutes to no more than an hour. In some cases, an image perspective can be used to illustrate a concept or present a theme to a client before the actual design process begins. In fact, there are many acceptable styles for image perspectives, from very loose and sketchy, to more refined; some styles even use drafted lines if they don't make the drawing appear too stiff and tight. These may be used for promotion or preliminary client presentation, and several hours may be devoted to their completion. Figures 8.2 through 8.9 are examples of image perspectives.

FINAL PERSPECTIVES

As shown in this book, a final perspective is the end result of the overlay method (see Chapter 12).

The visual appearance of a final perspective can vary greatly from project to project. Final perspective drawings may be black and white, partial color, or full color. They can be loose and sketchy or polished and photo-realistic.

Final perspectives are usually budgeted as an extra expense. When budgeting perspective drawing, time, size, style, and media must be considered. Unfortunately, the cost factor often negates the use of perspectives because these three-dimensional representations of design solutions can be so accurate that they are an invaluable tool in assuring clients that they are getting what they really want long before construction or the purchase of furniture begins. Conversely, if something needs to be changed it will be far more cost effective at this time, making the up-front cost of perspective drawings well worthwhile. Figures 8.10 through 8.12 show three versions of an image perspective for a science center.

For many years, final perspectives in black and white often relied on tight pen and ink drawings using more rigid mechanical methods. Today computers are playing an even greater role in perspective drawing, although they are still being used most often to wire frame the

PERSPECTIVE
DRAWING

Figure 8.2a

**IMAGE PERSPECTIVE, PENCIL, 8×10, 10 MINUTES—
RACQUETBALL CLUB DESIGN**

Figure 8.2b
**IMAGE PERSPECTIVE, PENCIL, 8 × 10, 10 MINUTES—
RACQUETBALL CLUB DESIGN**

KOENIG 80'

81

PERSPECTIVE
DRAWING

Figure 8.2d

**IMAGE PERSPECTIVE, PENCIL, 8 × 10, 10 MINUTES—
RACQUETBALL CLUB DESIGN**

KOENIG 80

Figure 8.3
IMAGE PERSPECTIVE, TWO-POINT, BASIC OFFICE DESIGN

Figure 8.4
IMAGE PERSPECTIVE FOR NATIONAL HIGH MAGNETIC FIELD LABORATORY LOBBY

PERSPECTIVE
DRAWING

with use of mech. line MOYA's ROOM

Figure 8.6
IMAGE PERSPECTIVE WITH FLOOR PLAN—HOUSE DESIGN

Figure 8.7
IMAGE PERSPECTIVE—HOUSE DESIGN

Figure 8.8
IMAGE PERSPECTIVE REFINED FROM THE ONE SHOWN IN FIGURE 8.7

PERSPECTIVE
DRAWING

Figure 8.9
IMAGE PERSPECTIVE, REFINED—HOUSE DESIGN

Figure 8.10
**FINISHED LEVEL PERSPECTIVE, BUT STILL CONFORMS TO
SOME IMAGE PERSPECTIVE RULES**

PERSPECTIVE
DRAWING

Figure 8.11

IMAGE PERSPECTIVE SKETCH—PROPOSED ODYSSEY SCIENCE CENTER

Figure 8.12

IMAGE PERSPECTIVE WITH A MORE FINISHED RESULT

PERSPECTIVE
DRAWING

drawing, which is then completed with hand rendering. The role of computers will continue to change as the rendering software becomes less expensive and more user friendly; their potential is limitless.

As a professional renderer, all of my final drawings are based on variations of the eyeball method with modifications to the overlay method. The drawings vary in style from quite loose to very polished in effect. The current trend is to take a simpler and freer approach in the teaching of rendering for design presentations.

Not much has changed in client-oriented presentations in the last 20 years. In most cases, full color renderings are still reserved for major commercial architectural projects. It is my hope, however, that designers will not lose the ability to draw and communicate at the presentation level and that books like this will remain part of design drawing education.

Section Three

··

DRAWING PROCESS

What is the drawing process?

The drawing process *for designers is critically linked to the* design process *for both problem solving and the presentation of the solution.*

In Chapter 7 we covered conceptual/doodle diagrams and image drawing and their role in the design process at the schematic or preliminary phase. Next we move into the design development or final phase of design where a variety of drawing choices are available to communicate the solution to the client. This level of drawing requires certain refinements that will take a proportionately longer span of time. At this point in the process, floor plans, lighting, elevations, furniture, and furnishing specifi-cations have been finalized.

Choices for drawing presentation type are still tied to time and budget. The perspective drawing is the most effective choice since it is pictural and easily understood by the client. Figures SK3.1 through SK3.4 were done while talking to a client in a meeting. At the presentation level, the designer may choose not to do his or her own perspective drawings but commission a professional renderer instead. This decision often depends on how valuable the designer's time may be doing other things and, of course, the cost may be charged back to the client. Although, comprehensive perspective

Figure SK3.1

**STUDY DONE WITH CLIENT, FLORIDA STATE UNIVERSITY
DISTANCE LEARNING CONFERENCE ROOM**

need door for
access

48×48

7'9"
Screen

35"
T.V.

4×6

VCR
Slide

?

move
Door
18"±

Cab.
35" TV.

T.V

②
Key bds → pull out
monitor

Figure SK3.2
**STUDY DONE WITH CLIENT, FLORIDA STATE UNIVERSITY
DISTANCE LEARNING CONFERENCE ROOM**

Figure SK3.3

**STUDY DONE WITH CLIENT, FLORIDA STATE UNIVERSITY
DISTANCE LEARNING CONFERENCE ROOM**

Figure SK3.4
STUDY DONE WITH CLIENT, FLORIDA STATE UNIVERSITY
DISTANCE LEARNING CONFERENCE ROOM

drawings may not prove to be cost effective in most residential situations, they are well worth the expense in commercial projects because they allow clients to see exactly what they are getting before construction begins, thus preventing changes that can be far more costly than the money invested in presentation drawings (Figures SK3.5 through SK3.7). Using logic in the drawing process—thinking through what to show the client and what drawing techniques to use—is essential at this stage.

This section discusses the overlay method, *beginning with composition studies and culminating in drawings suitable for client presentation. As previously explained, the scope of this discussion is limited to monochromatic—black and white—drawings. Most final drawings define color scheme solutions. Adding color is a valuable next step, and there are several good texts on the subject.*

The fewer surprises a client has on a given design project the less chance of negative response. Literally all relationships can be illustrated, from the simplest combination of furniture fabric patterns with adjacent floor textures to the most sophisticated architectural or lighting situations.

The overlay method allows the designer to customize the level of complexity and detail on a job-by-job basis to meet the needs of communication with individual clients. In fact, the designer can bring preliminary drawings to a client meeting and, using a tracing paper overlay, changes can be made while ideas are being exchanged.

Finally, the drawing process *allows the designer to express ideas at all phases of the* design process. *The client participates in the evolution of the solution, making meaningful changes along the way and giving final approval at the appropriate point of completion. These drawing and presentation skills give the designer great confidence in achieving client satisfaction long before construction begins.*

Figure SK3.5

**STUDIES DONE WITH CLIENT, FSU ACADEMIC
COMPUTER NETWORK SERVICES; PLAN AND PERSPECTIVES,
LOUNGE AREA**

LOUNGE

CORRIDOR

E.W.C.

vending

2 plants above

18"

2 garbage

30" table

FLOOR PLAN
ACNS

scale 1/4"=1'-0"
PK 1/14/99

Figure SK3.6

Figure SK3.7

ONE-POINT EYEBALL PERSPECTIVE

What is one-point eyeball perspective?

I differentiate the term eyeball perspective *from the term* mechanical perspective *based on the method and style used. In fact, the use of mechanical tools—T-square, triangle, and so on—has nothing to do with the term* eyeball; *the drawings may be entirely free hand or may be partially created with mechanical tools. This chapter demonstrates two distinct approaches to* eyeball *perspective* drawing.

The eyeball method is extremely valuable for quick sketch-type communication. Napkin art, *or a sketch done on a napkin during a lunch meeting, is this type of drawing. This type of sketch allows the designer to express ideas in perspective at a moment's notice without a need for a drafting table and tools.* Eyeball *methods can be used for image perspectives for in-house design or as an effective alternative to mechanical methods for final client-level perspectives. With the* one-point quick eyeball *method, the only critical variable is depth perception since this is always an educated guess. However, with the* eyeball method *this guesswork is eliminated by the use of a* vanishing point depth *(VPD). Certainly no eyeball* method is foolproof and, based on buzz words such as reality *and* believability, *changes that allow the drawing to better communicate always take precedence over grids and mechanical rules. The term* fudge factor *was developed by artists and renderers to give them license to adjust things in a drawing to make them appear more believable.*

One-point perspective works best for interiors since it allows the designer to show three walls of a space and concentrate on the focal point, or area of emphasis. There are two choices for overall page composition: full frame *(Figure 9.1), where the drawing extends to the picture plane, and* vignette *(Figure 9.2), where the four planes fade out equally on the paper.*

Figure 9.1
COMPOSITION, FULL FRAME

Figure 9.2
COMPOSITION, VIGNETTE

ONE-POINT
EYEBALL
PERSPECTIVE

ONE-POINT QUICK EYEBALL METHOD

No scale is used. The height or length of a line is merely what you say it is. Proportion is definitely the key to believability. However, all of the basic rules of perspective drawing should be used:

1. Pick the rear elevation of the perspective view. Include, at the left, a true height line (THL), which is the height of the space and to which the heights of everything in the drawing must be held.

2. Select the horizon line; approximately 3'6" or 5'6" is still appropriate.

3. Place the vanishing point (VP).

4. Select the sense of depth in the drawing. (This is a critical step since this is an educated guess and your practice with proportion is vital here.)

5. Use the x geometric method to divide and expand space. The x geometric method is based on the fact that drawing an x through a perfect square finds the center point of line. This principle carries over into perspective drawing with a square but vanishing plane. This method is extremely accurate if your *initial guess is a good one. (Remember: Heights and widths will always be accurate because you establish them as a given, but if your depth is off forms or furniture will clearly appear to be too foreshortened or extended.)*

EXPAND WALL X METHOD

EXTEND ROOM X METHOD

ONE-POINT
EYEBALL
PERSPECTIVE

EYEBALL METHOD

1. *Start at the rear elevation in your view of choice. Use an eight-foot ceiling height to prepare your grid. Use eyeball or draw to scale.*

2. *Draw the horizon line (HL) at 5'6" (or at 3'6" for a seated view).*

3. *Place the vanishing point (VP) to the left of center (or right depending on the emphasis of the view).*

4. *Place the vanishing point for depth (VPD) one and a half the width of the elevation from the VP. (This is an approximation and may vary.)*

5. *Draw a one-foot grid on the elevation.*

6. *Project the floor grid lines out from the VP.*

7. *Project lines from the VP through the rear elevation corner points to produce the wall planes.*

8. *Draw a diagonal line from VPD through point E to create point A.*

9. *Draw a parallel line from A to B, a perpendicular line from B to C, and a parallel line from C to D to complete the picture plane.*

10. *Draw horizontal lines at the points where the diagonal line EA intersects the floor vanishing lines; this produces a floor grid.*

11. *Now, using the VP from the elevation through the floor grid, draw the remaining wall and ceiling grids (Figure 9.3).*

Note: *The placement of the VPD is the critical factor that determines the proportion and/or distortion of the entire grid. It may be adjusted as needed. Also I suggest using a color such as red for guide lines—horizon line and VPD, E, A—since at completion of the method they may be removed, causing less confusion while using the grid.*

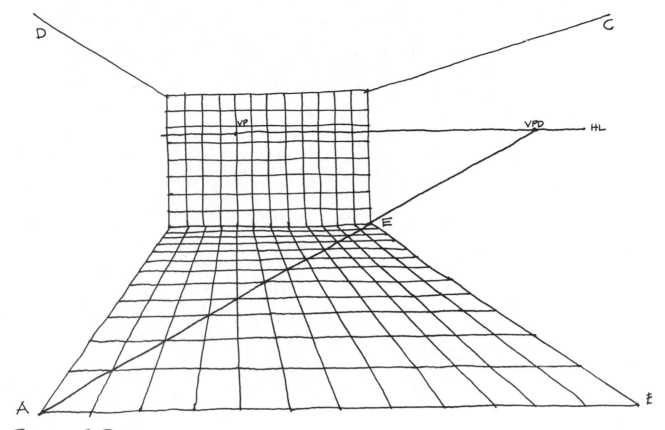

Figure 9.3
ONE-POINT EYEBALL METHOD, STEPS 1-11

Figure 9.4
CIRCLE IN PERSPECTIVE

ONE-POINT
EYEBALL
PERSPECTIVE

TWO-POINT EYEBALL PERSPECTIVE

10

What is two-point eyeball perspective?

Two-point perspective is ideal for viewing the corner or a more detailed view of a space since it cannot show the three walls of a space like one-point perspective can. Many believe that in certain spaces two-point perspective, even with its limitations, produces a more interesting or exciting view of the design. I prefer two-point perspective views to show exteriors of buildings.

Like one-point perspective, two point perspective also has both a quick eyeball *and an* eyeball method.

TWO-POINT QUICK EYEBALL METHOD

No scale is used. Once again, the height of the line is what you say it is. Basic rules for two-point perspective apply.

1. Pick the corner line of the view selected. This will be your true height line.

2. Select horizon line, approximately 3'6" or 5'6".

3. Place vanishing points on the left and right. The emphasis of the view will determine which is closer in.

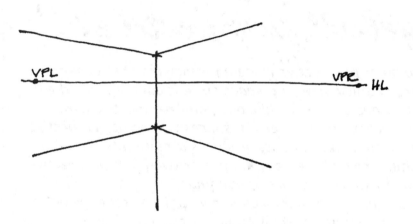

THL

4. Select your depth reference. Remember: This is still a guess.

5. Use the x geometric method to expand the space.

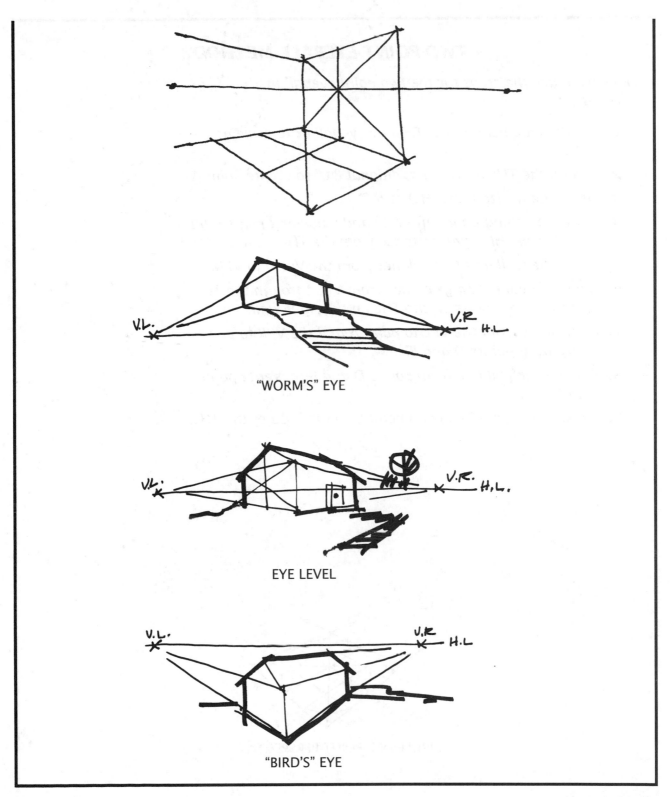

"WORM'S" EYE

EYE LEVEL

"BIRD'S" EYE

TWO-POINT
EYEBALL
PERSPECTIVE

TWO-POINT EYEBALL METHOD

Following are the steps for the two-point eyeball method (Figure 10.1):

1. Set the true height line (THL) by eyeball or to scale at 8′0″.

2. Extend the THL down an additional 8′0″ to create point A.

3. Draw the horizon line (HL) at 5′6″.

4. Draw vanishing point left (VPL) and vanishing point right (VPR) on the HL equal distance from the THL.

5. Draw the wall and floor planes from the VPL and VPR.

6. Draw the vanishing grid lines from VPL through the 1-foot to 8-foot points on the THL on the right wall.

7. Draw lines from the VPL to point A and the VPR to point A, creating points D and B.

8. Draw a vertical line from points D and B to create points E and C.

9. Draw a diagonal line from point C to the base of the THL.

.VPL   VPR.

CIRCLE IN 2-POINT PERSPECTIVE

10. Where the diagonal line cuts each vanishing wall grid line, drop a vertical grid line.

11. Draw the VPR floor grid lines.

12. Repeat the procedure for the left wall grid and complete the floor grid.

TO EXTEND THE WALL: Draw a diagonal line from the 4-foot point on the base of the wall through the 4-point on line BC to create point F, then drop new vertical lines at points cutting the vanishing lines.
Note: The placement of the VPL and VPR is critical to the proportion and distortion of the entire grid; you may adjust them as needed.

Figure 10.1

TWO-POINT EYEBALL METHOD, STEPS 1-12, PLUS WALL EXTENSION

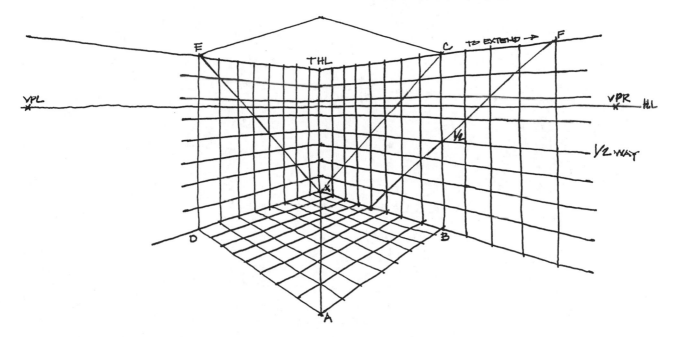

TWO-POINT
EYEBALL
PERSPECTIVE

COMPOSITION STUDIES

11

What are composition studies?

Composition studies play a vital role in developing a final-level perspective drawing for a client. Obviously, at this stage in the design process we already have a final floor plan, and the furniture and furnishings have been selected. At this stage the selection of a view that best communicates the design is critical, and a well-composed drawing allows the renderer to enhance it with tone/shadow, texture/materials, and color.

As part of the composition studies, some basic rules for good composition should be followed.

BALANCE

A drawing should always be in balance. The two basic types of drawing balance are symmetrical and asymmetrical which are basically the same as in the principles of design. A symmetrical composition is less dramatic or exciting than an asymmetrical one, but if the design is symmetrical then the drawing should be used to express this quality. Remember: If you are using figures in a drawing, they have visual weight and can be a positive factor in achieving balance.

Figure 11.1

BASIC PERSPECTIVE VIEWS EMPHASIZE CHANGES WITH MOVEMENT OF VANISHING POINT

EMPHASIS

This is the factor that determines how we express the visual impact and important features in the space. Here the term focal point *is used to indicate the strongest visual feature in the drawing or design. It may be a fireplace, a major piece of art, or some other important architectural or design feature. The focal point is usually found in the midground of the composition. If there is no specific focal point, a focal area may be indicated (Figure 11.1).*

POSITIVE OR NEGATIVE SPACE

The careful use of positive or negative space is essential to the balance of the drawing. Too much negative space in the composition can weaken the impact or throw the drawing out of balance.

DRAWING PROCESS **118**

FOREGROUND, MIDGROUND, AND BACKGROUND

Attention to these areas in a drawing will stimulate view-ers to move their eyes actively through the space. Fore-ground *is defined by any element, object, or form that penetrates the picture plane. We generally only think of foreground objects as being found in the lower front of a composition; however, they may be placed at anyplace around the perimeter as long as they penetrate the picture plane. The only critical decision is how much of an object to cut off, and this is generally based on proportion and the ability to still be able to identify the object. A drawing may still be effective without an actual foreground, but it can increase the believability that the viewer is in the space. The* midground *should be the strongest part of the composition since it should contain the focal point or focal area that enhances the empha-sis in the design. The* background *in the composition pro-duces the visual effect that carries the eye beyond the basic space shown, for example, looking out a window or into an adjacent space. Once again, in some compositions it may not be possible to use background as a feature but the end result can still be effective.*

These studies are a requirement when using the over-lay method (see Chapter 12). Time and budgetary constraints do not allow us the freedom to do unlimited perspective views. So limiting our composition studies, doing them quickly, in single line, and in small size is imperative. An eyeball method can save time, also draw-ing in line only, since at this time we are only concerned with building a strong composition that will serve as the foundation for the rest of the overlays. We will only be using one-point and two-point perspective alternatives, selecting standard 3' 6" or 5' 6" horizon line heights and typical vanishing point placements. However, there should be enough freedom in each design to select from composi-tional choices that best express its features.
Two to four studies are usually enough to make our final choice, although sometimes variations or combina-tions will be developed into the final composition. While working on the composition it is easy to use tracing paper

COMPOSITION
STUDIES

Figure 11.2
ONE-POINT COMPOSITION STUDIES

Figure 11.3
**TWO-POINT COMPOSITION
STUDIES**

COMPOSITION
STUDIES

Figure 11.4a
INTERIOR LIGHT WITH CONTRAST STUDY

Figure 11.4b
LINE WEIGHT STUDY

Figure 11.4c
TEXTURE STUDY

Figure 11.4d
TEXTURE, FOREGROUND OBJECT, OUT-THE-WINDOW STUDY

123

COMPOSITION
STUDIES

overlays in a preliminary manner to study various alternatives related to line, light, and texture with the use of more contrast. Or if there are challenging features such as views out windows, now is the time to experiment with them (Figure 11.4). On average, the size need be no bigger than 5" × 8" and a time frame of less than an hour is desirable. However, since a good composition is the foundation for all that follows, the time spent on these studies is well worthwhile.

OVERLAY METHOD

12

What is the overlay method?

The composition studies completed at this point provide us with the best view of what to show to communicate our design decisions to the client (see Chapter 11). These composition studies save valuable time in the long run and lay the foundation for a strong final result.

A good composition is by far the most critical part of a presentation drawing. In fact, compositional decisions should become second nature from the quickest sketch to a 20-hour rendering.

Once the best view provided by a one-point or two-point composition has been selected, we are ready to begin the overlay method. The term overlay refers to the use of tracing paper over a series of studies to arrive at an end result.

1. SINGLE LINE BLOW-UP

The first step is to convert the composition study to the size it will be for final presentation. The perspective may have been created by an eyeball method or a mechanical method (not part of this text). The style may be loose and sketchy or tight and controlled. You must be concerned with both line quality and weight in this single line drawing (Figure 12.1).

2. TONE/SHADOW STUDY

Place yellow or white parchment tracing paper over the single-line blow-up. *The media used for this can be pencil, pen, fine liner, or marker. Now select your light source: natural, artificial, or a combination.*

Figure 12.1

**OVERLAY METHOD—
SINGLE-LINE BLOW-UP**

First apply your tones, starting with the broad planes: walls, floor, and ceiling. Remember: The most successful values move from 0 to 10, or white to black. Be sure to save your black for the shadows. **Note:** Do not retrace your lines; use tone only (Figure 12.2).

Next apply the shadows. Since these are studies, do them as quickly as possible and feel free to experiment with your light sources. You should never experiment on a final drawing; now is the time. Shadows can be strong, bold, and geometric in style or soft and subtle; you be the judge in each drawing.

Figure 12.2

OVERLAY METHOD—LIGHT STUDY, TONE/SHADOW

Since you don't want to just color in between the lines, creating what I call the coloring book *effect*, you can often use two tones meeting to create the line, thus eliminating the redundant *line*.

Most beginners are not nearly bold enough with tone and shadow. It is a good idea to back away from the drawing and look at it from a distance, to check the visual impact. This is still one of the easiest areas to improve upon.

3. TEXTURE/MATERIALS

Once again, place your tracing paper over the line drawing for this overlay. All of the elements in a space have texture; this study will help you decide what to emphasize in the drawing (Figure 12.3). Since drawing texture and materials can be very time consuming, you can use techniques to let the eye of the viewer complete some of the imagery for you. There are many entourage books that include a variety of real and generic textures for your use. However, since there is no single correct way to create texture, you may feel free to develop your own method; whatever works is right.

Remember that texture is an element of design that can create visual interest and stimulation. It can give a space its character from rustic to hi-tech. It affects the design principles of unity and variety.

4. THE FINAL PERSPECTIVE DRAWING

This is the sum total of the best of your overlay studies (Figure 12.4). The drawing will be part of your client-oriented presentation. The end result is often tied to budgetary constraints and time. Generally, only major-scale projects have money allocated to this type of drawing. This is a shame since in the long run the information these drawings convey will inevitably save money when changes must be made.

The umbrella that defines final drawings is very broad. Sketch styles vary from tight and mechanical, black and white, full or part color, and vignette to full frame. All of the examples of my final drawings shown

Figure 12.3
**OVERLAY METHOD—TEXTURE/MATERIALS
STUDY**

here are *eyeball* or a variation thereof. The size, complexity, and medium usually dictate the cost.

A good final drawing can assure clients that they are getting what they want. The role of the renderer is to portray the design as accurately as possible and be as flattering as we can. But we must not misuse our skills just to please through the many tricks of the trade; to be fair to the client, we must maintain our integrity through the use of this art form.

Figures 12.5 through 12.10 are examples of preliminary and final perspective drawings.

Figure 12.4

OVERLAY METHOD—ALL STUDIES COMBINED INTO FINAL DRAWING

Figure 12.5a
**PRELIMINARY STUDY FOR
FLORIDA A&M UNIVERSITY
DINING HALL**

Figure 12.5b
**REFINED STUDY FOR FLORIDA A&M UNIVERSITY DINING
HALL**

Figure 12.6

FINAL PEN AND INK STUDY FOR FIGURES 12.5A AND B.

Figure 12.7a
STUDY FOR PEGASUS RECORDING STUDIO

Figure 12.7b
DETAIL OF FIGURE 12.7A

133 OVERLAY METHOD

Figure 12.8

**FINAL PEN AND INK RENDERING FOR
PEGASUS RECORDING STUDIO**

PEGASUS STUDIOS

DRAWING PROCESS **134**

Figure 12.9

**FINAL PEN AND INK RENDERING OF
A RESIDENCE**

Figure 12.10

FINAL PEN AND INK RENDERING OF A MARINA

ENTOURAGE FOR FINAL DRAWINGS

13

Entourage was first defined in Chapter 5 as the many elements that humanize a final drawing and add a sense of believability to the perspective. Many of these things allow us to use the skills we learned in free-hand sketching, which adds a nice loose touch to the drawing.

HUMAN FIGURES

The human figure in final presentations, in both residential and nonresidential projects, can play an important role. However, in residential presentations they often pose a real dilemma, for unless we use truly generic figures we can face the pitfall of trying to draw the figure to resemble the client. This can create some potentially embarrassing situations. In nonresidential or commercial projects, on the other hand, using figures can show the space functioning and bring it to life. Figures can play a basic role in establishing a stronger composition. They are a strong source of form, and a vertical figure can have the visual weight of a column in both interior and exterior views. Triangulating the placement of figures from the foreground to the midground to the background provides a sense of scale and an illusion of depth perception in the composition (Figures 13.2 through 13.6).

   Avoid using large foreground figures in the center of the front. Since they will need to be perfectly drawn, they may distract the viewers' attention from the rest of the space or block important features. Even worse is using a large foreground figure from the rear view. Also stay away from poses even an accomplished artist would avoid, for example, a figure seated front face (Figure 13.1).

Figures should appear as if they belong in the space, placed in poses that would appear natural for the scene shown. Since most people find drawing the hands and feet to be the most difficult, I recommend that you group figures or place them in relationship to furniture in ways that a minimum of these body parts are visible. Tracing figures from an entourage book is an acceptable method, but care must be taken since the authors of such books usually have excellent drawing skills. Perfectly tracing

Figure 13.1

FIGURE PLACEMENT STUDY USING TRIANGULATION, ON YELLOW TRACING PAPER

Figure 13.2
FIGURE PLACEMENT STUDY

Figure 13.3
TRIANGULATION

139 ENTOURAGE FOR
FINAL DRAWINGS

their figures may make them stand out in your drawing for a variety of reasons. Here are several suggestions for avoiding this pitfall:

1. Draw your own figure directly next to the one in the book.

2. Trace the figure, then retrace your tracing several times (Figure 13.5). This will allow you to express some of your own line character and style, thus making the figure fit more naturally into your final drawing.

3. Change a part of the original pose by moving an arm or leg, once again adding something of your own to the figure's character.

4. Finally, select up-to-date hair styles and clothing and be sure the figures are appropriately dressed for the space you are designing. A figure overlay study may be extremely valuable.

Figure 13.4

AVOID A LARGE FOREGROUND FIGURE

DOS

DONT'S

Figure 13.5
TRACING OF FIGURES

Figure 13.6

FIGURE AND ENTOURAGE STUDY

ENTOURAGE FOR
FINAL DRAWINGS

Figure 13.7a
**EXTERIOR SKETCH WITH
ENTOURAGE**

Figure 13.7b

REFINED EXTERIOR SKETCH WITH ENTOURAGE

ENTOURAGE FOR
FINAL DRAWINGS

TREES AND PLANTS

You have by this time practiced sketching real trees and plants from life, studying their growth patterns and how light affects them. Plants play a vital role in interior design and using real plant varieties in your drawings makes them more believable. Interiors that have windows need to maintain the drawings' horizon line and express a true sense of the exterior view. Generally, the value and detail of the scene and objects outside should be muted and have less detail since the designer wants to keep the viewers' attention on the interior spaces. Although reality is important, proper use of generic textures for planting can be both effective and, sometimes more importantly, time saving (Figure 13.8).

Figure 13.8

EXTERIOR PLANTING AND MATERIALS

line quality test grass/ground cover effect

145   ENTOURAGE FOR
FINAL DRAWINGS

Figure 13.9

BLOW-UP FROM RESIDENTIAL RENDERING

STUFF

Options for adding accessories to a drawing are unlimited, so be creative. Once again it is advisable to work from real objects or good photographs rather than working from memory. Select objects carefully, from a telephone to a table setting, since attention to detail is the strong point of the most believable drawings. These accessories usually cannot be drafted and are free form, allowing your line quality and sketching skills to add a nice touch to any final drawing.

ART

Art is an often critical part of a residential or commercial design (Figure 13.10). It is best to not try to make your drawing of art work too literal. In many cases, the final

Figure 13.10
SKETCH WITH ART

ENTOURAGE FOR
FINAL DRAWINGS

art has not been chosen at the time of your presentation. Therefore, placing the right type of art for the space is as important as figure selection. For example, one would not expect a realistic landscape painting in a high-tech interior. Basically, keep the wall art or sculpture simple; give it character without too much detail. Entourage is the last thing added in the overlay method, but it may well be the most important. Viewers are most comfortable with things they recognize. The humanizing aspects of these objects can go a long way in your communication to the client. The design solutions you have presented through your drawings will reinforce their decision in selecting you to creatively solve their problems (Figure 13.11).

Figure 13.11

TWO-POINT IMAGE PERSPECTIVE WITH ART AND ACCESSORIES

PRESENTATION

14

What is presentation?

Presentation is the method we use to display our design drawings to the client. Presentation and its success or failure has absolutely nothing to do with your ability to draw or design. Of course, successful presentation skills will certainly prove beneficial to the designer, while mistakes in judgment or craftsmanship will have a negative or distracting factor.

In the past, the most popular method of presenting design drawings was to mat them. This is a time-consuming and often very expensive presentation method.

Basically, the best method of presentation is often the simplest. In fact, drawings may simply be mounted directly to a backboard or presented on individual sheets of paper that may be protected with a lamination process and later placed in protective folders in the portfolio. However, using strip mats on either the top and bottom or bottom only is still popular and far more economical.

Mats are used to frame the drawings and contain the eye, creating a more formal and finished look. Two critical factors in matting are proportion and color. Proportion varies as it is directly related to the size of the

149

drawing. Based on optical illusion, the bottom section of a mat should always be slightly larger to maintain visual balance. When choosing a color for a mat, be sure to place a sample of the board next to your drawings to get the correct value and intensity.

Neutral mat colors are usually the best choice; in fact, a white or black mat or possibly a value of gray is preferable with a black and white drawing. Also, if warm or cool markers are used in the drawing they will determine the color of gray selected for the mat. Use caution when selecting a black mat since it may overwhelm a subtle drawing.

Colored mats will likely distract from a monochromatic drawing. Although color is not the subject of this text, matching the color of the mat to a color in the drawing is recommended. You do not need to match the exact color; instead choose the value and intensity of the color that works best to set off your work. Although presentation methods have not changed much in the past few years, there has been a trend toward simplification: projects and portfolios are smaller, and less matting is used on drawings.

Following are some key concerns in presentation:

1. **Craftsmanship.** This is vital since sloppiness can affect the attitude of a client toward all of your work. Drawings that are not spaced evenly or have poorly cut mats are clearly distracting to the viewer.

2. **Composition.** Compose and balance your boards and use implied margins as needed. This not only aids in continuity but makes complex drawings more easily defined and readable.

3. **Title information.** Select title information and style carefully. Typeface selection and size are very important for emphasis. The placement of written information helps with balance and emphasis. Be consistent with centering and right or left margins.

4. **Consistency in presentation.** Place the boards in a consistent direction, either vertical or horizontal. Also be consistent with your choice of media, which may be mixed. Develop a consistent drawing style.